Acknowledgments

The Bible verses in the *5-Minute Bible Devotionals* series were selected from the following Bible versions:

Scripture quotations marked NIV are taken from the Holy Bible, New International Version®. NIV®. Copyright © 1973, 1978, 1984 by International Bible Society. Used by permission of Zondervan. All rights reserved.

Scripture quotations marked NASB are taken from the New American Standard Bible®. Copyright © 1960, 1962, 1963, 1968, 1971, 1972, 1973, 1975, 1977, 1995 by The Lockman Foundation. Used by permission.

Scripture quotations marked NKJV are taken from the New King James Version. Copyright © 1982 by Thomas Nelson, Inc. Used by permission. All rights reserved.

Scripture quotations marked KJV are from the Holy Bible, King James Version (Authorized Version). First published in 1611.

Scripture quotations marked RSV are taken from the Revised Standard Version of the Bible, copyright © 1946, 1952, 1971 by the Division of Christian Education of the National Council of the Churches of Christ in the USA. Used by permission.

Scripture quotations marked TLB are taken from The Living Bible, copyright © 1971. Used by permission of Tyndale House Publishers, Inc., Carol Stream, Illinois 60188. All rights reserved.

The Bible verses that are noted as "paraphrased" are taken from *Feed My Lambs—Bible Verses for Kids Made Fun*, by Derek and Michelle Brookes, © 2002 by Aurora Production AG, Switzerland. Used by permission. All rights reserved. Adaptations to the verses were made to simplify the vocabulary for young children while retaining the original meaning, and were based on the King James Version in consultation with several translations of the Bible, primarily the New King James Version® and the New International Version®.

Author: Katiuscia Giusti

Illustrations: Sabine Rich

Design: Chris Martin

ISBN: 978-3-03730-638-3

© 2012 Aurora Production AG, Switzerland.

FEED MY LAMBS

5-MINUTE
BIBLE DEVOTIONALS

FOR YOUNG CHILDREN

In this book you will find:

15 devotionals for preschool-aged children

Each devotional based on a **Bible scripture**

An **activity** for each devotional

Topics in this book:

Faith

God's Promises

FAITH THAT GROWS AND GROWS

Faith comes by hearing the word of God.

—Romans 10:17, *paraphrased*

God wants us to learn to trust Him. But sometimes it can be hard to trust when we do not know what is going to happen. The Bible says that our faith will grow as we read and study God's Word. When we read the Bible we learn of the many times that God did amazing things for those who trusted in Him and believed His promises.

We can experience miracles too! God's promises are true. If we study what God has said about His love and care for us, then we can trust and believe that God will take care of us and provide for us. He loves to answer our prayers and show us that He is a loving and caring God.

The more we study God's Word, the stronger our faith in God grows.

Can you think of a story in the Bible where a miracle took place because someone had faith in God's mighty power?

TRUST JESUS

Trust in the Lord with all your heart, and do not lean on your own understanding.

—Proverbs 3:5 NAS

Jesus is like our loving father who takes good care of us. We can trust Him to provide for us, just like we trust our parents to look after us. Wouldn't it be silly if we told our daddy and mommy that they didn't need to take care of us anymore, and that we could now do it ourselves? When we are little, we need our parents, and everyone needs Jesus' loving care.

Jesus wants people all over the world to trust Him and to let Him help them. But sometimes we think we know how to do things without Jesus, so we don't ask for His help. It makes Jesus happy when we trust Him to care for us.

When we trust Jesus, we don't have to worry about anything, because we're in Jesus' loving care.

Take a few moments to thank Jesus for how wonderfully He cares for you.

"Thank You, Jesus, for Your love. You take such good care of me, and I'm thankful that I can trust You. Help me to remember to come to You whenever I have a need rather than trying to do it all on my own. I trust You! Amen."

NOTHING IS IMPOSSIBLE FOR JESUS

According to your faith
it will be done for you.

—Matthew 9:29, *paraphrased*

Learn this little rhyme:
I believe God's Word is true;
There is nothing He can't do.

The Bible tells us the story of two men who were blind. They went to Jesus to ask Him to heal them so they could see.

"Do you believe that I can do this miracle?" Jesus asked the men.

"Yes, Lord," they replied.

Jesus then told the men that because they had faith in His power, He was able to heal them. And suddenly the two men could see!

When we have faith in Jesus and in His power, many wonderful things can happen for us. It can be hard to believe in something that seems impossible. But always remember that nothing is impossible for Jesus. He's the great God of the universe, and will do miracles for us when we believe.

God is powerful!

OUR AWESOME PROTECTOR

God has not given us a spirit of fear, but of power, and of love, and of a sound mind.

—2 Timothy 1:7 NKJV

Have you ever had to face something frightening? Maybe you are afraid of thunderstorms and the loud thunderclaps. Or maybe you feel scared of the dark. It doesn't feel nice to be afraid. When we are frightened by something, we want someone to save us from whatever it is that we're scared of.

Jesus can be our protector whenever we face something frightening. It doesn't matter what we are afraid of, when we turn to Jesus and ask Him to keep us safe, He will do just that. Jesus can give us peace that will help us to feel the comfort of His love in our hearts.

We can talk to Jesus about our fears, and then we can trust that He will keep us safe. We don't have anything to worry about when Jesus is taking care of us.

Draw a picture of Jesus watching over
you, and then draw a circle around you
and Jesus. This is the place where Jesus
is keeping you safe from the things that
may make you fearful. Talk about some
of the things that you would like Jesus
to help you to not worry about.

WHEN WE BELIEVE

A man once came to Jesus and asked Him to heal his son who was very sick. Jesus told the boy's father that anything was possible if he believed and had faith in God's power. The man asked Jesus to help him believe completely. Because of the father's faith, Jesus performed a miracle, and the boy who was sick was healed.

All things are possible if you believe.

—Mark 9:23, *paraphrased*

Jesus can still do miracles for us today if we have faith and believe in His power. It doesn't really matter how big the problem is, when we ask Jesus in faith, He can do something fantastic, just like He did many times throughout His life on earth.

Can you think of another story in the Bible where Jesus worked a miracle because someone had faith in God's power?

We can show our faith and trust in Jesus through our prayers and belief that He can do miracles for us. This makes Jesus happy.

LOOKING AFTER US

Fear not, for I am with you;
I am your God, I will strengthen
you and help you.

—Isaiah 41:10, *paraphrased*

God is wonderful and powerful! He is so amazing! And what is even better is that He has promised that when we believe in Him, then we can ask Him for His help and strength, and He will give it to us.

When we know and love God, then we don't need to be afraid of things that we face. That doesn't mean that difficult things won't happen to us, but it does mean that even if we need to do something difficult or that makes us feel afraid, we simply have to remember that God is with us. He will look after us. He will give us the courage that we need and show us what to do.

Isn't it wonderful to know that God is there for us? That should make us feel very safe, happy, and loved, because the amazing God of the whole universe is looking after each one of us.

Ask your mommy or daddy to write out the words "God always takes care of me" on a piece of paper. Now decorate your page however you like. Then when you're done, post it by your bed or in your room so that you can remember God's love and care.

PERFECT PEACE

You will keep him in perfect peace whose mind is fixed on You, because he trusts in You.

—Isaiah 26:3, *paraphrased*

Sometimes we are afraid. When we are afraid, we may not know what to do to make the fear go away. Jesus can help us. Jesus doesn't want us to be afraid. He wants us to be happy.

When we're afraid we can tell Jesus what is troubling us, and then we can ask Him to fill our hearts with peace. It doesn't matter how big or how small our fears are, we can talk with Jesus about them, and He will comfort us.

So whenever we are fearful, we can think about Jesus and His love and care for us. We trust Jesus because He will take care of us and will protect us. Jesus brings peace to our hearts when we trust in Him.

Learn this rhyme to recite
whenever you're afraid:

Jesus, whenever I am afraid,
I can always talk to You.
You give me perfect peace
That nothing can undo.

WITH JESUS' HELP

I can do all things through Christ who gives me strength.

—Philippians 4:13, *paraphrased*

Little jobs can be done by little people. Sometimes, though, we need to do a bigger task that may seem too hard for us. Maybe it's a chore we have never done before, or we're still learning how to do it right. It's important not to give up when something is new or seems difficult at first.

Here's a little secret: Jesus can help us do big jobs too. Jesus promises that He will help us to do all things. If something seems too hard for us to do, we can ask Jesus for His help.

Jesus can give us the patience to learn something new, especially when we may have to try our new skill a few times before we know how to do it well. When we ask Jesus for His help, and then do our best, we are able to learn many new and wonderful skills.

Learning is an exciting part of growing up, and Jesus wants to help us in all that we do.

Here is a simple rhyme you can recite whenever you are learning something new:

When a job is too hard for me,
And I don't know what to do,
With Jesus' help I can do all things–
Oh, this I know is true!

MAKE JESUS HAPPY

Delight yourself in the Lord and He will give you the desires of your heart.

—Psalm 37:4 NIV

Can you think of some things that make Jesus happy when we do them? Are they always easy to do? Some things are probably hard to do, but it is important to keep trying.

Can you think of a time when you really wanted something special? Maybe your mommy and daddy told you that if you did your chores diligently you could get that special toy. You may have found it difficult to remember to do your chores and to do them well, but once you did, you were rewarded.

The Bible says that when we do our best to please Jesus and do those things that are right, then He can bless us. And when Jesus blesses us, He not only gives us the things we need, but even the things we want, if He knows they will be good for us.

It is not always easy to be obedient to our parents, to be truthful, to be thoughtful of others, but when we do those good things, we make Jesus happy. As we make Jesus happy, He makes us happy too.

JESUS LEADS US

In all your ways acknowledge the Lord and He will direct your paths.

—Proverbs 3:6, *paraphrased*

Have you gone somewhere new with your parents, and did they have to ask others how to get there? It probably took time to stop and ask someone for directions, but those directions were important because they helped your parents find the way.

We often need to ask others for help. Maybe we are facing a new challenge and need some help, or we are looking for something and cannot find it, or we are learning something new and need someone to teach us how to do it. Not only can we ask others for help, but we should also learn to ask Jesus for His help. This way He can show us what to do.

No matter what we are doing, when we stop to listen to Jesus, He can speak to our hearts and tell us the right way to go. Then, as we follow and obey Him, we will find that Jesus leads us to good and happy places.

Pretend that you are having a conversation with Jesus on the phone because you need to ask Him for help. Your mommy or daddy can pretend to be Jesus. Stop and listen to what He has to say.

ALWAYS BY OUR SIDE

I will never leave you
nor forsake you.

—Hebrews 13:5 NKJV

Have you ever been lost and couldn't find your mommy or daddy? It can be frightening when you are lost.

Even in situations when we are lost or afraid, Jesus is always with us. Jesus tells us in the Bible that He will never leave us. That means that wherever we are in the world, whatever situations we face, Jesus is always right there with us.

Jesus is our forever friend. He is with us in whatever we do. He's promised to look after us and care for us, His children. So if we ever feel alone or are frightened, we can remember that Jesus is with us. He is our protector and our friend, who never leaves our side. Isn't that wonderful?

Draw a picture of you and Jesus doing something together. Ask your mommy or daddy to write the verse "I will never leave you nor forsake you" on your picture. Put it by your bed or desk to remind you that Jesus is always with you.

NO MATTER HOW BIG

My grace is sufficient for you, for My strength is made perfect in weakness.

—2 Corinthians 12:9 NKJV

Pretend to be lifting something heavy, and then ask your mommy or daddy to help you lift it and move it for you. Talk about something you're learning that is hard for you or that you may have trouble remembering to do. Then say a prayer asking Jesus for His help.

Have you ever tried to move something heavy, and no matter how much you pulled and pushed it, it simply wouldn't budge? Then maybe your daddy came along and helped you move it, and you were very happy for your daddy's help.

As children we are learning many things, and some of the things we have to learn about, like obedience, caring for others and things, or being courteous, can be difficult. But whatever we are learning to do to build good character and strong spirits, we can always ask Jesus for His help. Then, just like a strong daddy will help us lift a heavy load, Jesus will give us a hand, and that makes it easier for us to do those things that can seem so hard to do or learn.

If we stop and pray and ask Jesus for His help to do those things that we know are right but which might be difficult for us, He's always happy to work with us. It doesn't matter how big the problem is or how difficult it might seem to us, Jesus is bigger and better than all of it!

WHEN WE DON'T KNOW WHAT TO DO

If you lack wisdom, ask God,
and He will give it to you.

—James 1:5, *paraphrased*

Sometimes we need to make choices, but we don't know what will be the best thing to choose. Then, the more we think about the choices, the more difficult it is to decide which one will make us and others the happiest, and we don't know what to do.

The Bible says that God can give us wisdom. Wisdom is what helps us to make good decisions, even difficult ones. When God gives us wisdom, we don't suddenly become very smart and know all the answers. Instead God's wisdom leads us, and guides us to the best choices—the ones that will make us the happiest and that will make God glad, too.

It doesn't matter how big or small our choices are, we can always pray and ask God for His wisdom. Then as we stop to listen, He will show us what the best choices are.

Pick out one of your toys to hide, then ask your mommy or daddy to put a blindfold on you. Once you are blindfolded, your parent can hide the toy in the room, and you then need to try to find it with the blindfold on. (Walk carefully!) After you try that for a little while, with your blindfold still on, ask your mommy or daddy to hold your hand and lead you to find the toy. When you have found the toy, take your blindfold off. Then talk about how much easier it was to find the toy when you had someone to guide you, and how God is always there to help us no matter what we need His help to do.

ALL OUR NEEDS

God will supply all your needs.

—Philippians 4:19 NASB

The Bible tells us many amazing stories about the times that God supplied for His people. Like the time the prophet Elijah needed food and God sent ravens to bring him food twice a day. Or the time when Moses and the children of Israel were in the desert and needed water, and God told Moses that water would come from the rock, and by a miracle that is what happened. Water came rushing from the rock—enough for everyone to drink.

Many times throughout history God has done miracles to supply the things His children needed. And even today, God still does miracles for us. When we have a need, we can ask God to supply it for us, and He will answer our prayers. It makes God happy when we look to Him when we have a need. We may not always receive the answer right away, but God will answer our prayers when He knows it is best for us. He likes to answer our prayers. God will take good care of us!

Can you think of other stories in the Bible when God supplied for His people?

EVERYTHING TURNS OUT ALL RIGHT

All things work together for good for those who love God.

—Romans 8:28 NKJV

On a piece of paper draw a swirling scribble. Now color in each of the spaces of the scribble with a variety of colors, until everything is colored in. What once looked like a scribble is now a pretty and colorful illustration.

When a friend has to leave, when we have been sick, when we have problems, those events don't look good to us. In the Bible we learn that because we love Jesus and believe in Him, even when things don't seem to go well, or difficult things happen to us, we can trust that they will work out for good in the end. That means that we have faith that some day we'll be able to see something good come from what has happened.

Maybe you planned to play at the park, but it started to rain and you had to stay inside. The rain at first seemed liked a "bad thing," but you still had fun, because you found something enjoyable to do inside instead.

There are many ways that good can come from the things that at first seem bad. Jesus knows how to make everything turn out all right.

A WORD TO THE PARENT

"Do you love Me?" Jesus asked Peter.
"Lord, You know all things," Peter answered. "You know that I love You."
"Then feed My sheep," Jesus said. "And take care of My little ones."

—Based on John 21:15–17.

5-Minute Bible Devotionals is a collection of Christian and character-building books written for children ages four on up. Each devotional is built on a Bible verse, and explains to a child in simple terms what the principles of that verse mean and how it applies to daily living.

I wrote these books to provide opportunities for conversation and discussion on Christian values between parent and child on a level that is relatable to a child. You can simply select a devotional to read with your child and pause when questions are posed in the text to allow time for your child to answer. Then encourage your child to express personal experiences or thoughts that relate to the theme you are reading.

Included with each devotional is a simple activity, such as a discussion question, a short rhyme to learn, or a simple project. I have found that emphasizing the lesson I am teaching my children by means of interactive activities brings that spark of fun into the mix that makes these important times of learning a joy.

The Bible verses included with each devotional have been selected from a variety of translations or revised so that they are easy for a young child to understand. Children can also be taught these verses. Repeat the verse several times with your child; he or she should soon be able to recite it from memory. Make a point to review the verses a couple of times a week so the child retains what has been learned.

In addition, I will often spice up a devotional reading by including related Bible or character-building stories that complement the principles being taught.

My aim for these books was to have a way to teach my young children Bible-based values, and I have had a wonderful time sharing these simple truths with them in this way. It is my hope that you'll experience the same.

Katiuscia Giusti

5-MINUTE BIBLE DEVOTIONALS

Collect the full series!

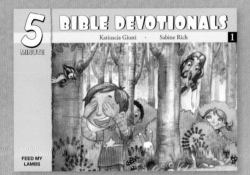

Love • Salvation

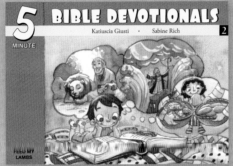

Faith • God's Promises

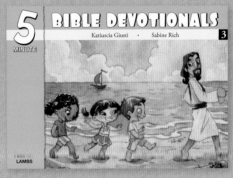

Prayer • God's Word

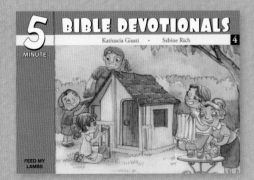

Christian Living

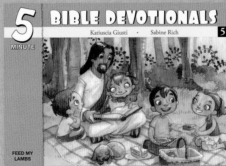

God/Jesus • Following Jesus • Obedience
Forgiveness

Holy Spirit • Preach the Gospel • Healing
God's Power in You